Positive Affirmation Coloring Book for Adults

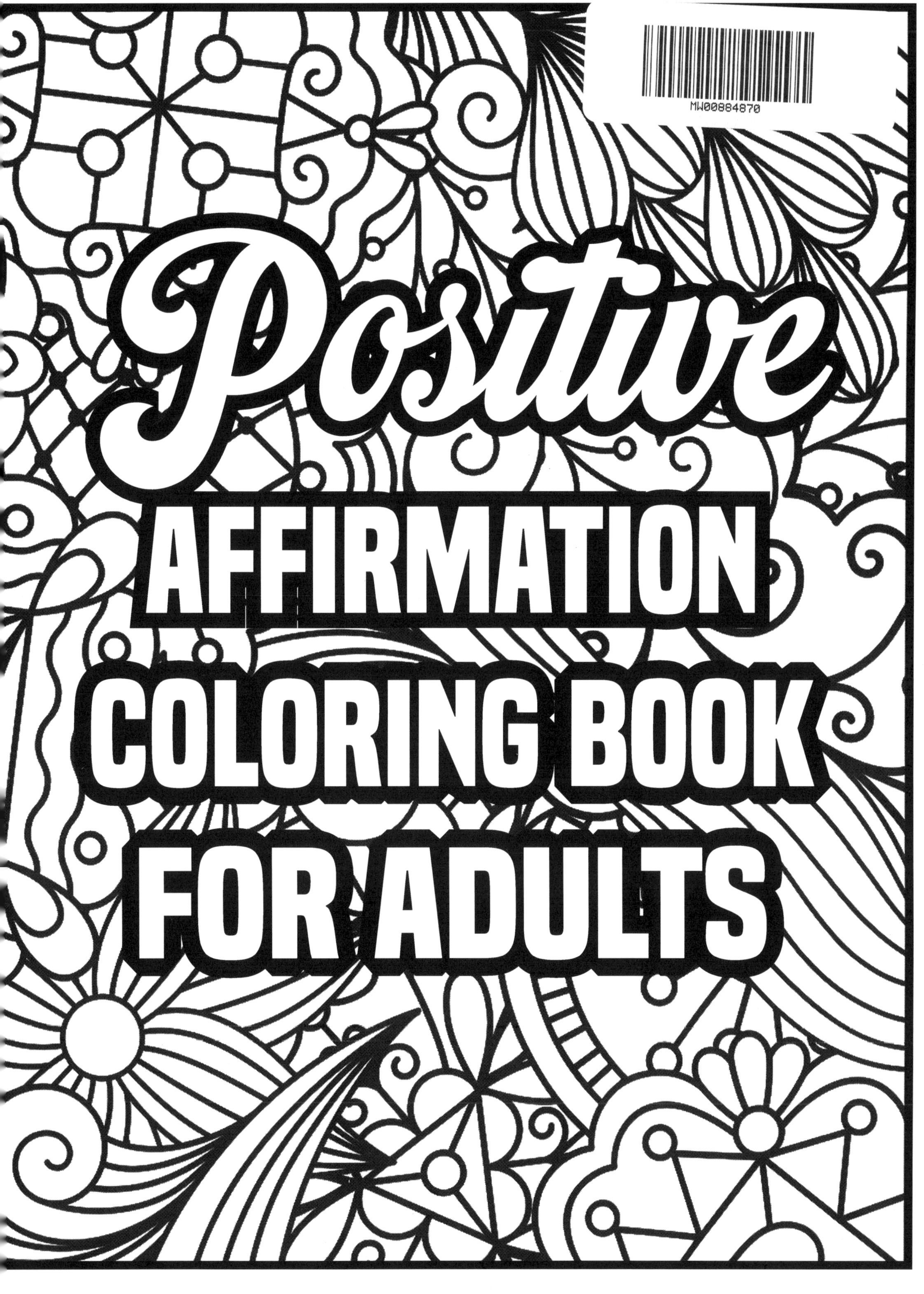

This book belongs to…

Color Test

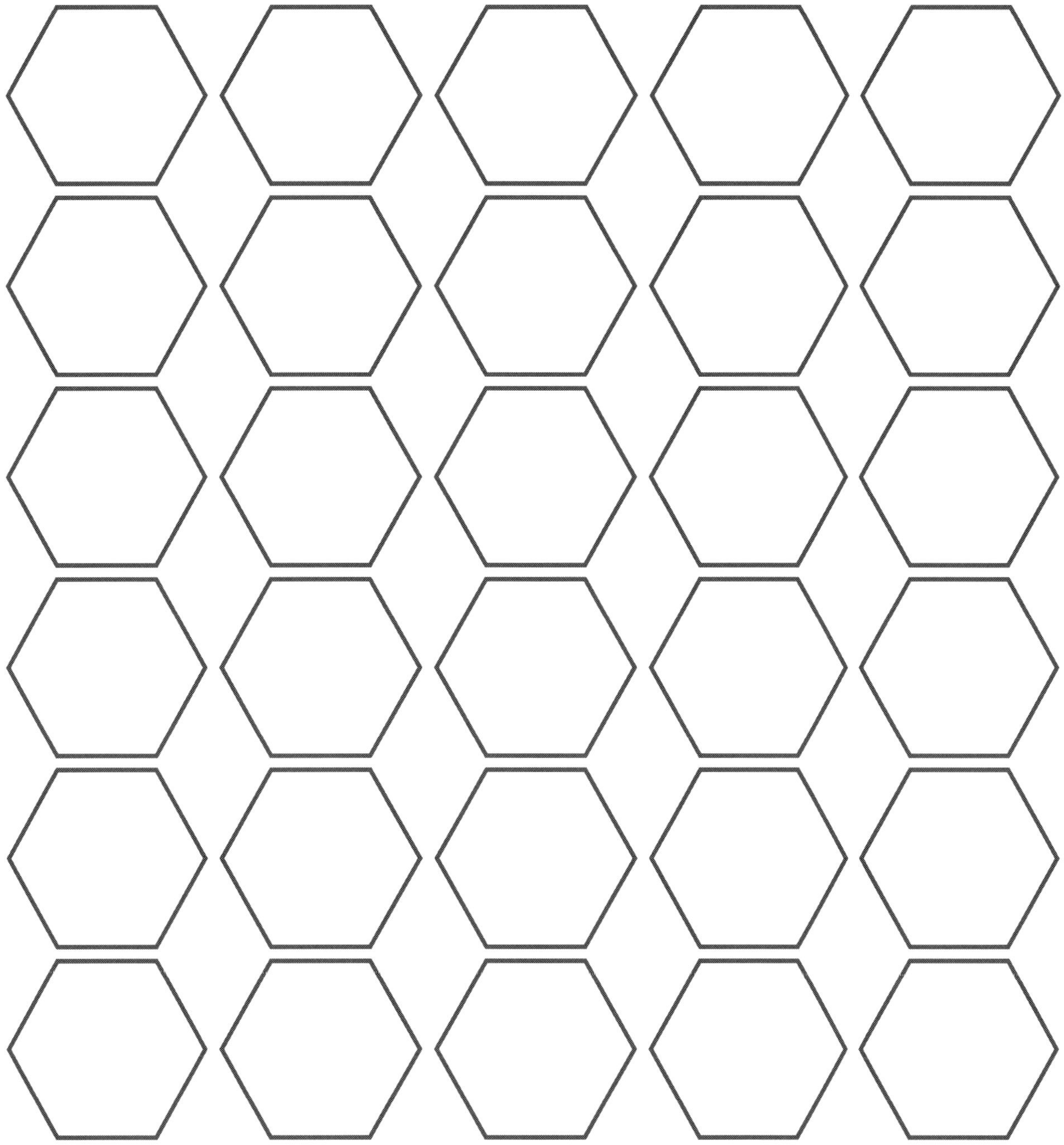

BE YOU
Do You
FOR YOU

ONCE YOU
Realize
YOUR WORTH
Nothing
CAN STOP YOU

YOU ARE
Capable
OF AMAZING
Things

GET OUT
Of Your
OWN WAY

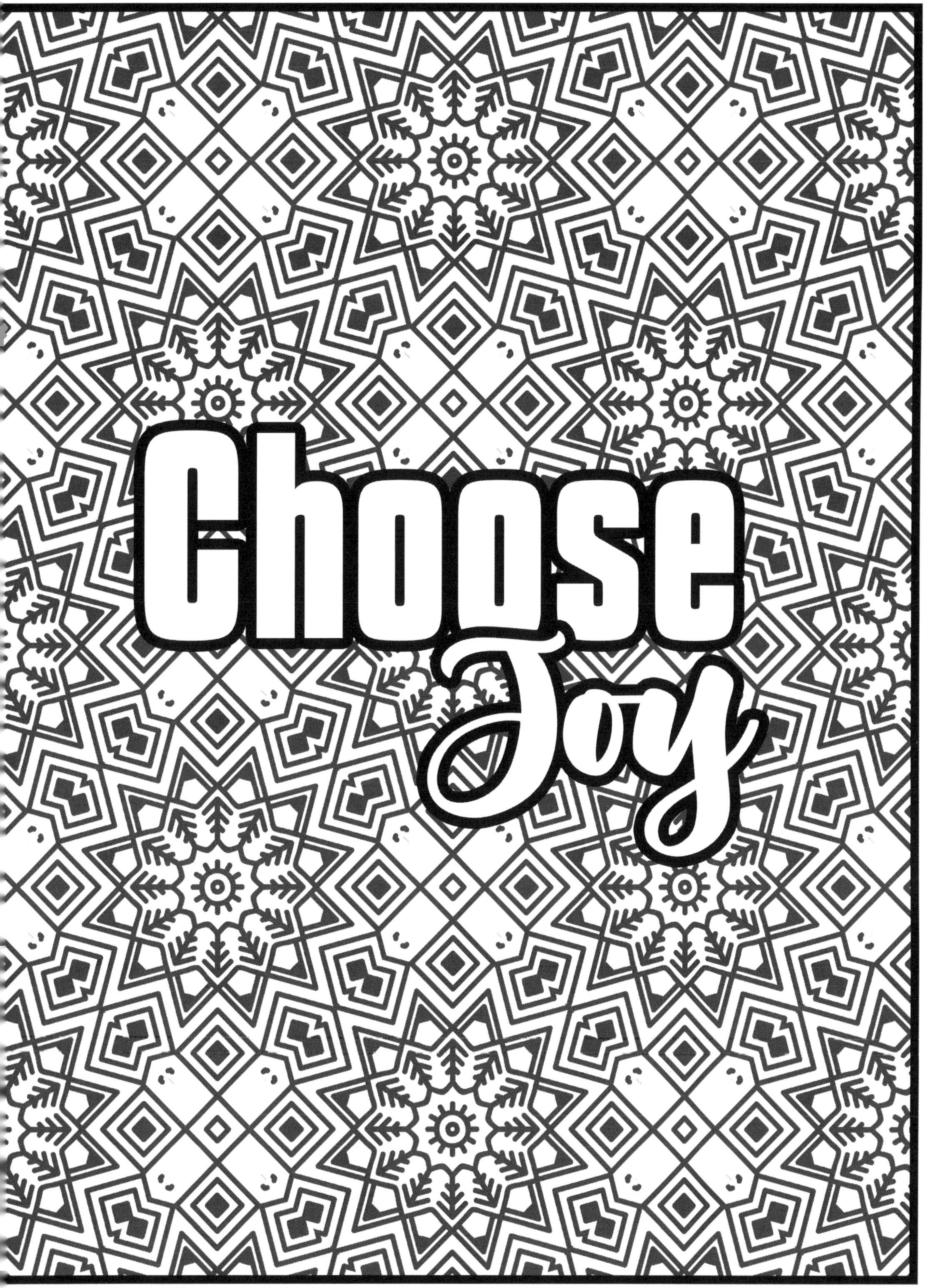
Choose
Joy

COLLECT
Moments
NOT THINGS

BELIEVE
There Is
GOOD
In The
WORLD

ALL THINGS
Are Difficult
BEFORE
They Are
EASY

AND
So The
ADVENTURE
Begins

NEVER
STOP
Dreaming

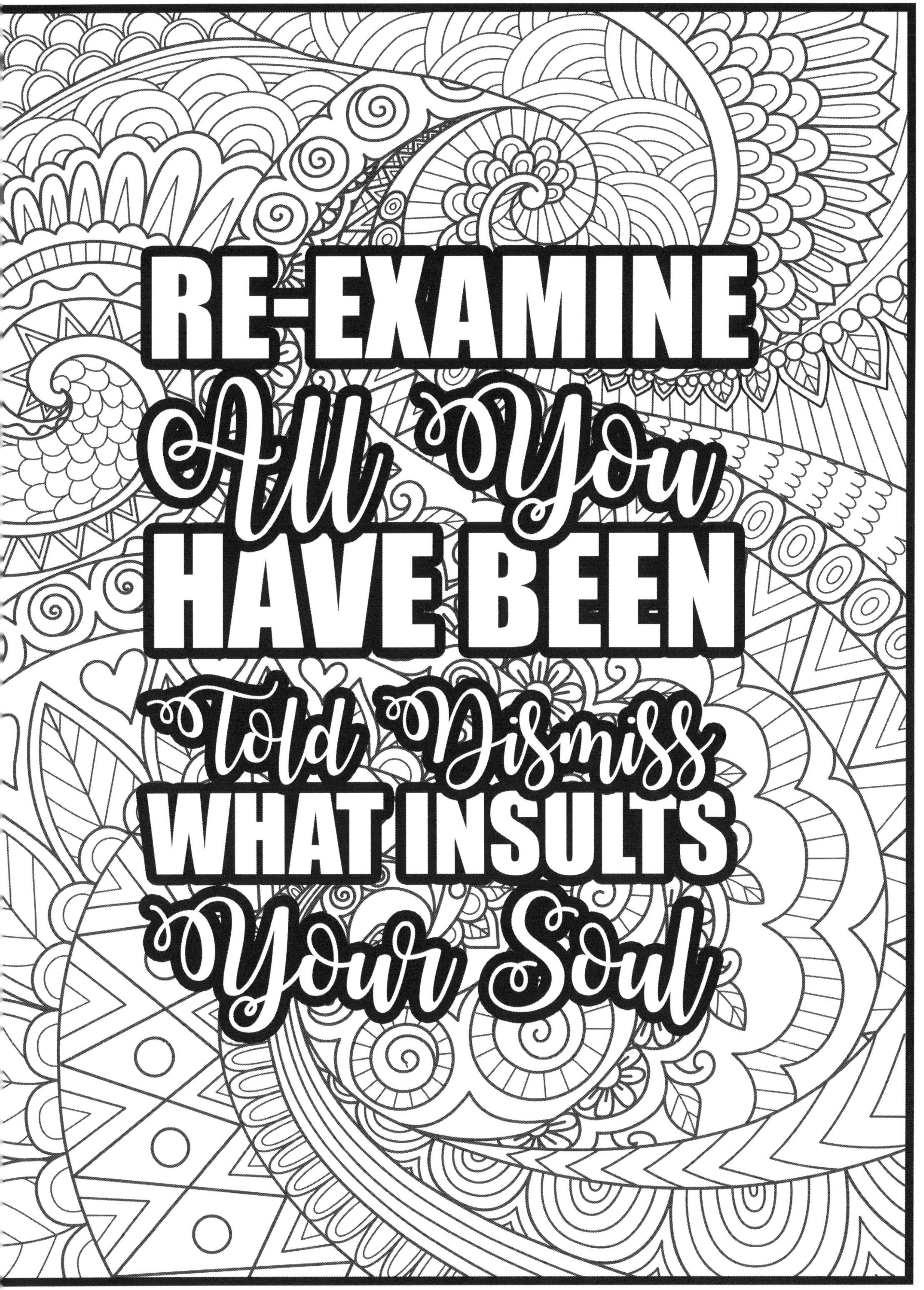
RE-EXAMINE
All You
HAVE BEEN
Told Dismiss
WHAT INSULTS
Your Soul

DREAM
Without
FEAR

TODAY
Is A
BRAND
New Day!

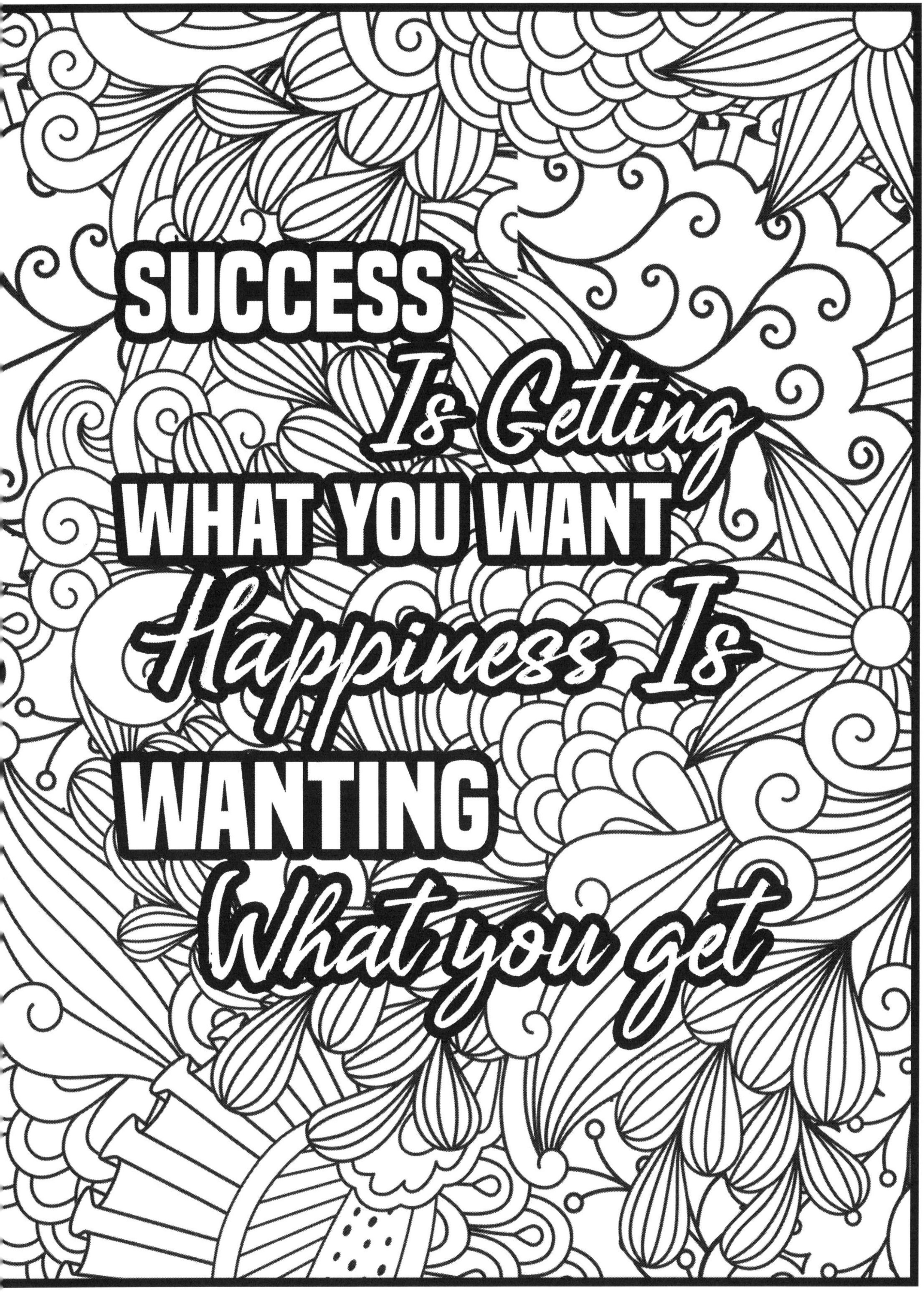
SUCCESS
Is Getting
WHAT YOU WANT
Happiness Is
WANTING
What you get

NEVER
Stop
LOOKING
Up

BE
Obsessively
GRATEFUL

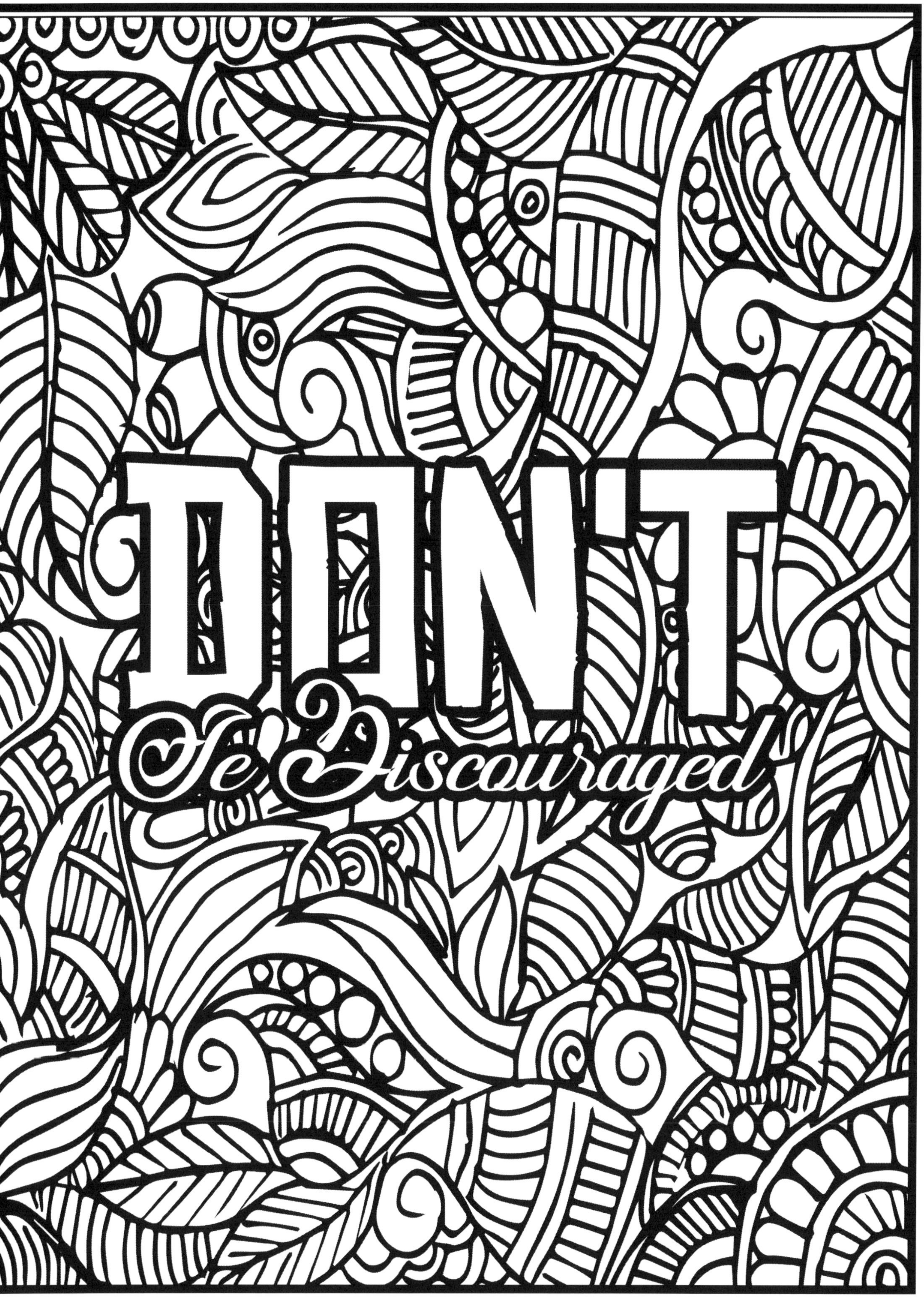
DON'T
Be Discouraged!

BEING
Kind
NEVER GOES
Out Of
STYLE

THE BEST
Version
OF YOU

WORK
Hard
STAY
Strong

WHEN
One Door
OF HAPPINESS
Close
another opens

HARD TIMES
Like These
MAKE US
Stronger

DO RIGHT
Even
WHEN NO ONE
Is Watching

DON'T
Wait
FOR BETTER
time

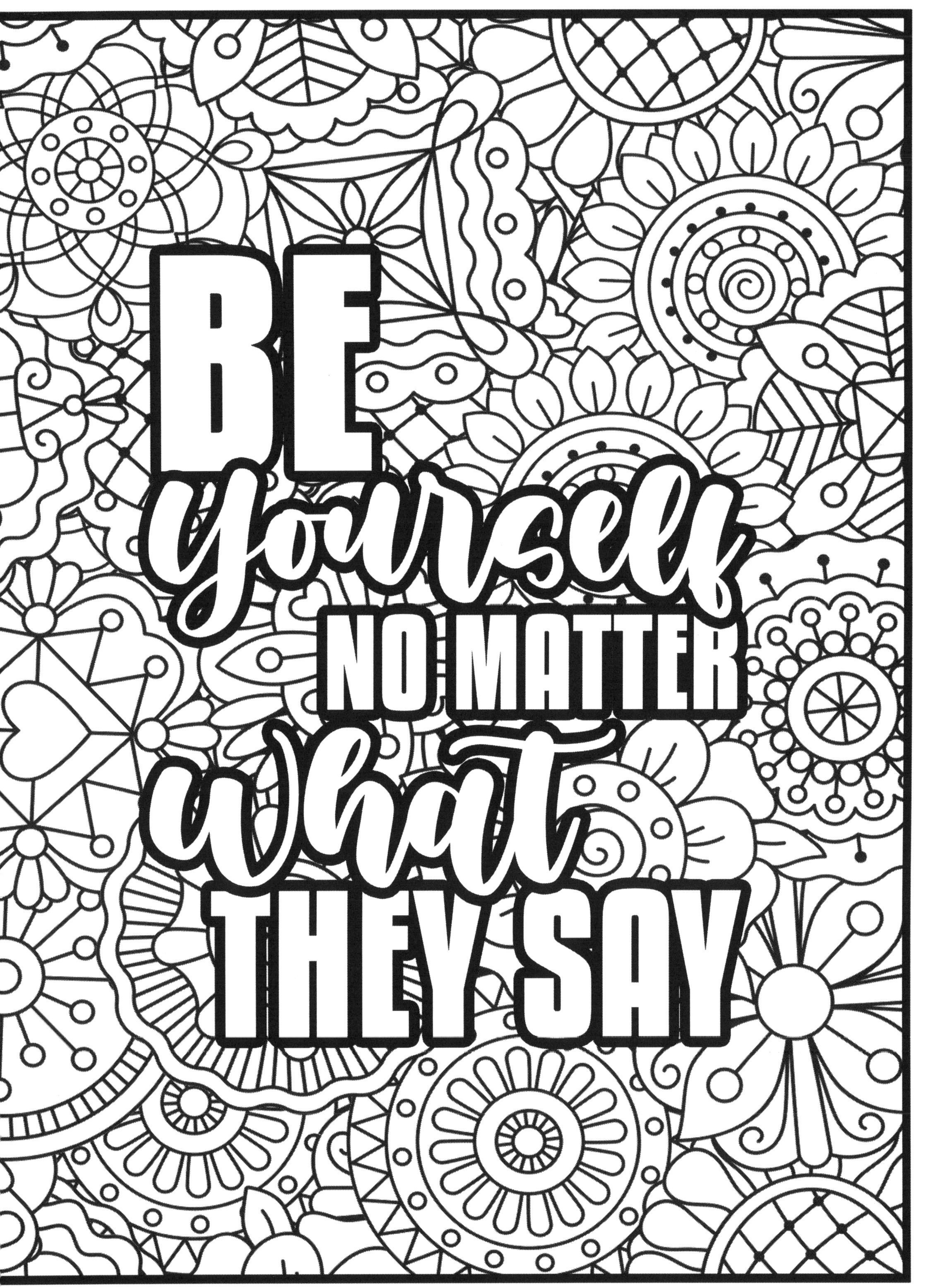
BE
yourself
NO MATTER
what
THEY SAY

BEAUTIFUL
Minds
INSPIRE
Others

PUSH
Yourself

DARE
To Be
DIFFERENT!

THE
Best Day
IS TODAY

DON'T
Let Yesterday
TAKE UP TOO
Much Today

NEVER
Let Your Emotions
OVERPOWER
Your Intelligence

PASSION
Over
PERFECTION

YOU
Are The
FUTURE!

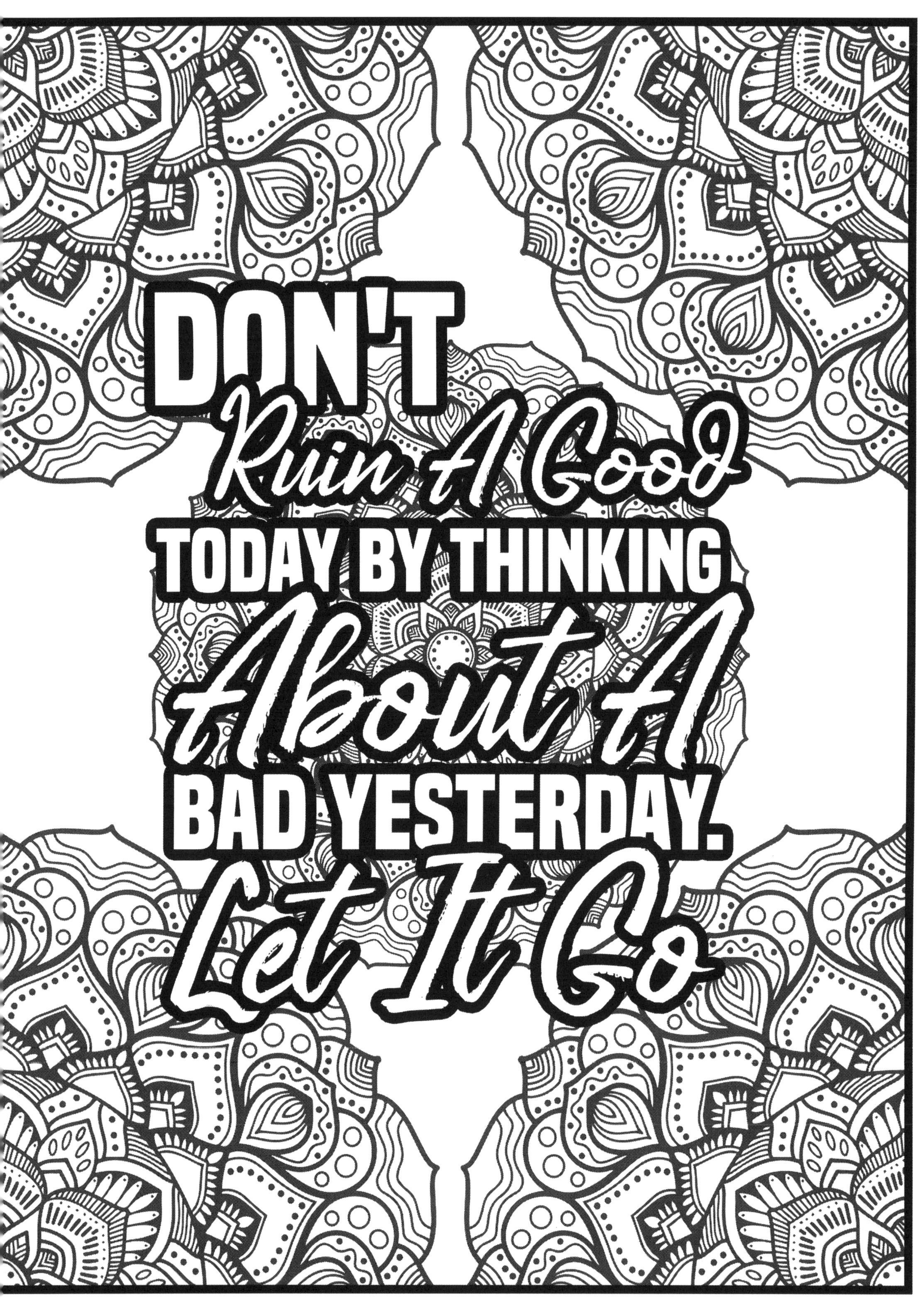
DON'T
Ruin A Good
TODAY BY THINKING
About A
BAD YESTERDAY.
Let It Go

BE
The Best
VERSION
Of You

STAY FOCUSED
Stay Positive
NEVER
Give Up

GIVE YOURSELF
Permission
TO REST

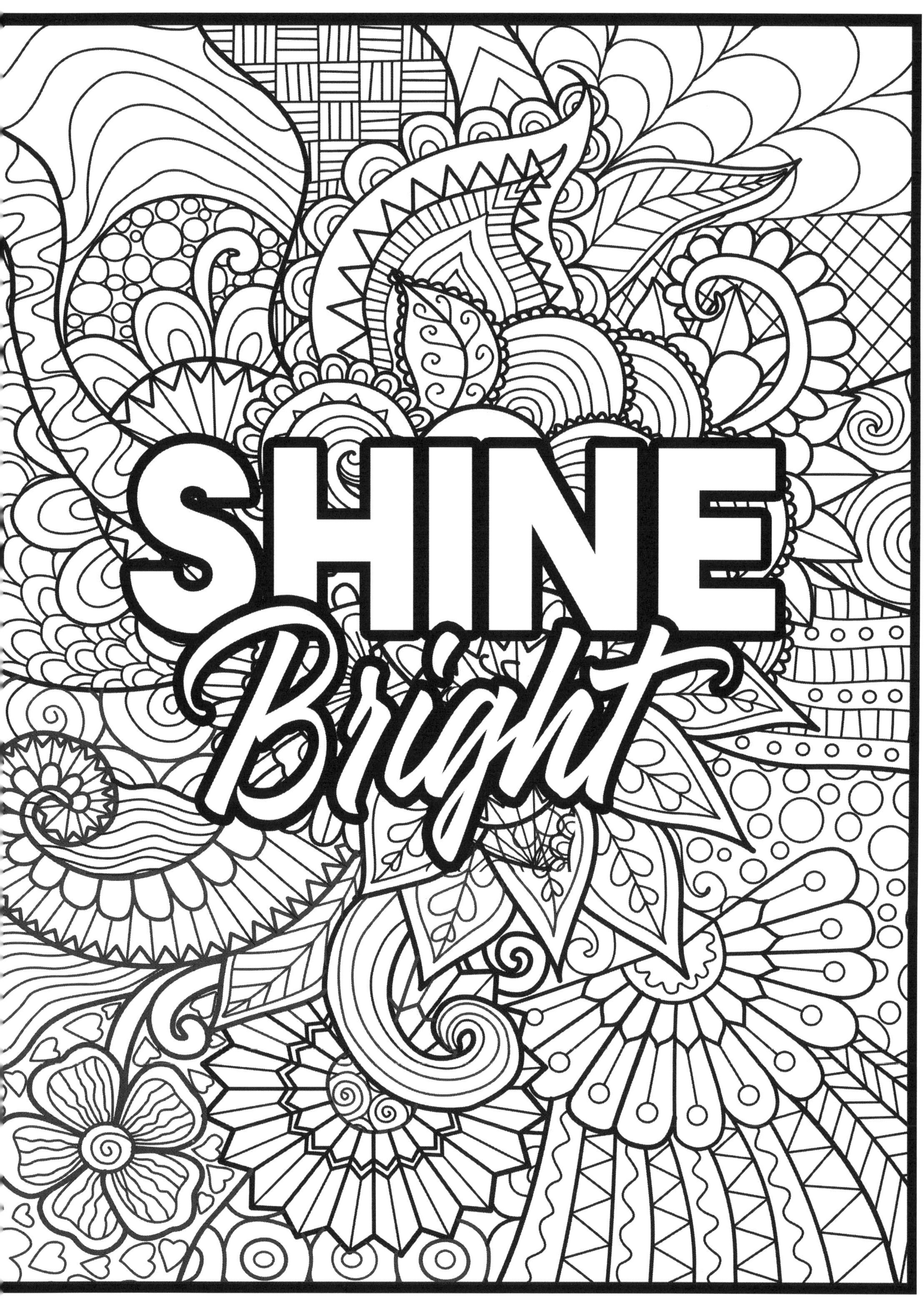
SHINE
Bright

DO
More
OF WHAT
Makes You
HAPPY

DO
what you
LOVE
LOVE
what you
DO

EVERYDAY
Is A
FRESH
Start

CALM
And smile
ON

GREAT
& Hustle

TODAY
Is Going
TO BE
Awesome

LISTEN
more
SPEAK LESS

CHOOSE
To Be
GRATEFUL

THE BEST
Dreams
HAPPEN
When Youre
AWAKE

CHOICE
Chance
CHANGE

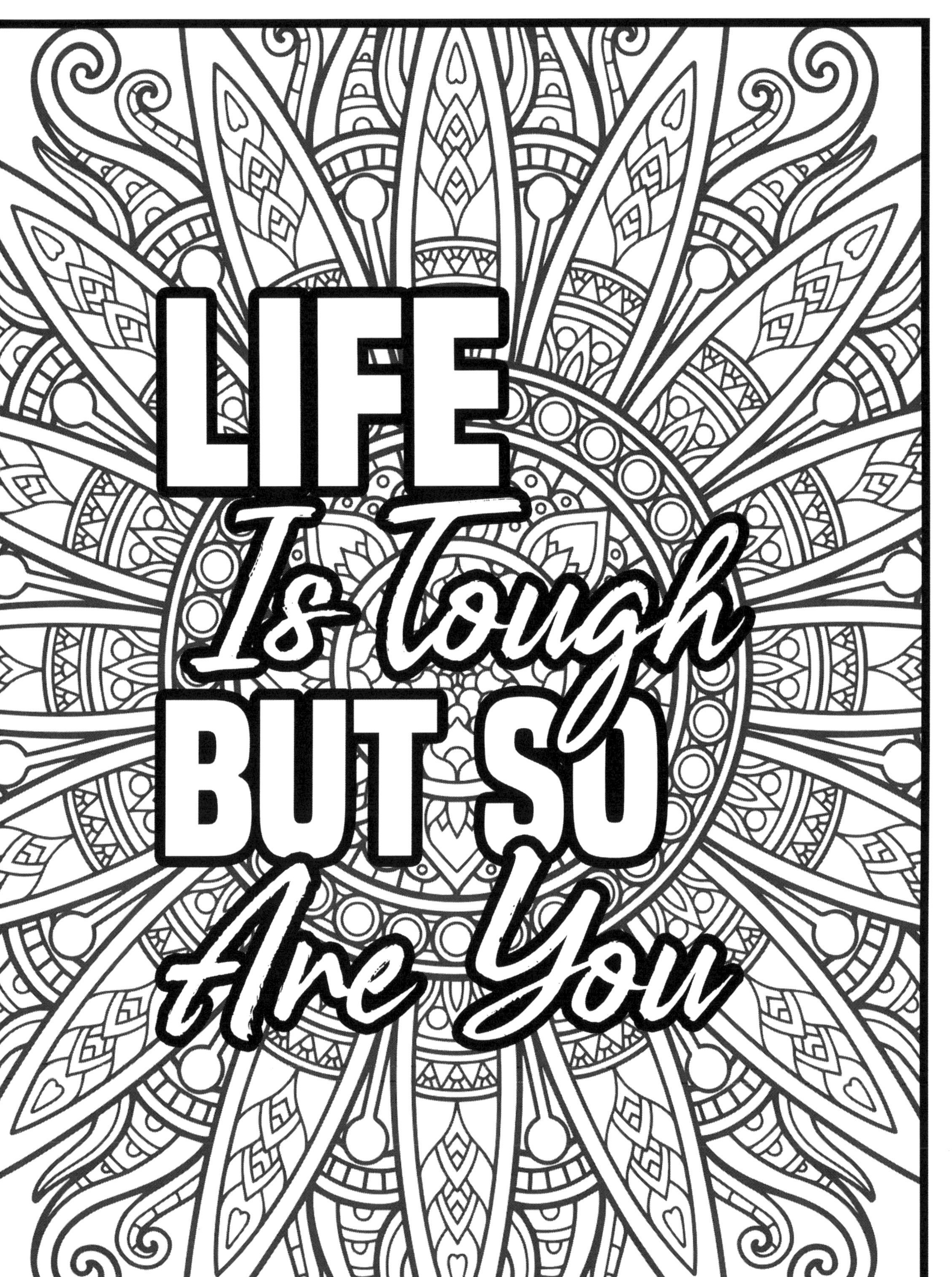
LIFE
Is Tough
BUT SO
Are You

A HERO IS
Someone
WHO HAS GIVEN
His Or Her Life
TO SOMETNING
BIGGER THAN
Oneself

Made in United States
Orlando, FL
16 July 2024

49034414R00061